THE FLEETING KARATE MASTER

富名腰義豪

FUNAKOSHI GIGO

Translated by Eric Shahan

FUNAKOSHI GIGO・富名腰義豪

The Elder Teacher Gichin is the type who succeeds through effort, the Young Sensei Gigo succeeds through sheer innate ability.

FUNAKOSHI GIGO・富名腰義豪

Table of Contents

富名腰義豪
Funakoshi Gigo
(1906 ~ 1945)

Funakoshi Gigo was the third son of legendary martial artist Funakoshi Gichin (1868 ~1957) who was one of the first Okinawan Karate practitioners to introduce their art in mainland Japan.

Funakoshi Gigo, whose name was pronounced Yoshitaka on mainland Japan, was born in the 39th year of Meiji (1906) in Naha, Okinawa. His father had four sons, and gave them all names that used the first Kanji of his name "Gi" 義 meaning righteousness, duty and honor. His children were Giei, Giyu, Gigo and Giketsu. His fourth son Giketsu, passed away at a young age and following the path of martial arts did not appeal to his second son, Giyu. His eldest son, Giei, who had been encouraged to do martial arts from a young age by his father, took lessons at the Dojo of renowned Okinawan Karate Jutsu practitioners Asato Anko and Itosu Anko, becoming a Karate practitioner of considerable skill.

Gigo was diagnosed with tuberculosis and was therefore somewhat frail, but began training Karate at around the age of twelve in order to improve his health.

In Taisho 15 (1926,) when he was seventeen years old, his father asked him to move to Tokyo. Initially, Yamada Tatsu[1] found Gigo had a job selling for a lumberyard in Fukagawa, however thanks to the goodwill of two of his father's students, Himono Kazumi and Matsuda Shoichi, Gigo was able to train for a job in the medical field. He became an X-ray and radiation therapy technician at the Physical and Medical Consultation Section of the Ministry of Education.[2]

As Funakoshi Gichin was now in his late fifties, most thought that Funakoshi Giei would be the one to succeed his father as head of the Shotokan, however Giei himself, inspired by Gigo's passion, recommended his younger brother to the position.

---

[1] Yamada Tatsuo 山田辰雄 (1905~1967)

[2] Himono Kazumi 檜物一三 and Matsuda Shoichi 松田勝一 were doctors. In 1925, while attending medical school at Tokyo Imperial University they founded the Tokyo Imperial University Karate Research Society 東京帝国大学唐手研究会

The reason was a difference in character. Later, many students of Gigo commented,

The Elder Sensei (Gichin) is the type who succeeds through effort, the Young Sensei (Gigo) succeeds through sheer innate ability.

Kaku Kozo 加来耕三
Interesting Historical Japanese Fighting Arts Stories
日本格闘技おもしろ史話 1993

Hironori Otsuka recalled how Gigo Sensei made the transition from medical technician to full-time martial arts instructor.

Gigo was taught how to be a radiation technician by Himono Kazumi and was able to pass the test to get qualified. Therefore, young Gigo owed a great debt to Himono Kazumi...Young Gigo started doing Karate at the suggestion of his elder brother Giei, who arrived in Tokyo after him. After Young Giei arrived in Tokyo he began working as a shop assistant at a shop in the Ministry of Finance building. I told both of them that as their father was getting on in years, they both needed to work together to get Gigo ready to take over as successor.

So Gigo came up with a plan to take a month off and return to Okinawa for intensive Karate Jutsu training. Three weeks after he returned, he quit the radiation clinic and became a full time Karate Jutsu instructor. This was probably around the time we were using the Masago Dojo.

-Hironori Otsuka 大塚博紀 (1892 ~ 1982)
Before and After the Meisho Juku Era
明正塾前後 1977

Egami Shigeru, who joined the Waseda University Karate club in the 8th year of Showa (1933,) notes that most people at the Dojo referred to Gigo as Waka Sensei, the Young Teacher, to differentiate him from his father, referred to as Roshi, the Elder Master Teacher. Egami's description of Gigo Sensei

Gigo Sensei's legs were thin and Kani-mata, a little bowlegged like a crab, overall, he was rather undistinguished looking. However, when he put on his white technician's uniform, he became a friendly and caring hospital staff member. On the other hand, when he put on his Karate uniform, he became such a severe Sensei that it seemed he was another person entirely. I was startling to see and I wondered where he concealed that intensity and fighting sprit when not at the Dojo.

- Egami Shigeru (1912~1981)
Lessons Left Behind by Elder Shoto Sensei
郎師松濤先生の遺訓

Reporter and author Togawa Yukio (1912~2004) was an early member of the Shotokan Dojo and trained with both Funakoshi Gichin and Funakoshi Gigo. He described the different approaches to training used by these two Karate masters.

Gichin Sensei was elderly and primarily focused on teaching Kata, at night Gigo Sensei used a scientific approach to teaching the fundamentals and overall focused on how techniques could be applied practically. Gigo Sensei was Gichin Sensei's third son and, at the time, his ability as a Karate practitioner were second to none. I even thought,
This man is what they talk about when they say someone is a master of their art.
Thus, I tried to train with Gigo Sensei as much as I could, and I even skipped work at the newspaper company to attend evening training.

-Togawa Yukio
Memories of the Shotokan

Egami Shigeru notes that Gigo Sensei felt it was imperative to train other martial arts and master the techniques that were taught. Thus, Gigo Sensei also studied weapons like Bo (wooden staff) and Ken (sword) in addition to Judo. He used Bo techniques to help train Tai Sabaki, body movement in reaction to attacks.

> He would wrap a bit of cotton cloth around the end of a pole and hand it to one of his students and order them, "Strike me as hard as you can!" The fact that his forehead often had large welts on it is an amusing episode to recall.
>
> -Egami Shigeru

In an interview with Kamata Toshio (1918~2018) Hosokawa recalled an episode where he sparred with Gigo Sensei

> Gigo Sensei ordered Kamata, *Tsuite Koi! Strike at me!*
> Kamata launched a Chudan Tsuki. Gigo Sensei responded by stepping in and sweeping Kamata's foot in a flash. Everyone watching went *Ah!* worried about what would come next, but pulling back from the jaws of certain defeat, Kamata used his rear leg to pivot around and returned to his original spot, meaning his technique had stayed intact.
> Gigo Sensei laughed and praised Kamata saying,
> *I doubt there are more than a handful of people in Japan that could pull of that technique.*
>
> -Kamata Toshio
> *Karatedo Monthly* 月間空手道 January 1957

Up until Showa 9 (1934) the head instructor under Funakoshi Gichin was Shimoda Takeshi (1901~1934.) Unfortunately, he passed away at just thirty-three years old. Shimoda Takeshi, who was a dental technician by trade, also studied Ninjutsu as well as Maniwa Nen Ryu, a school of sword, halberd and spear founded in 1591. He began training under the Funakoshi Gichin and, in a relatively short time, he became a standout student, in fact he was referred to as *Ippon Sugi*, a Pine Tree that Stands Apart, or a student head and shoulders above the rest. He was known for having a round belly and always wearing Japanese style clothing.

Egami Shigeru recorded some of his impressions of Shimoda Sensei and his martial arts technique,

> Shimoda always had a warm, inviting smile on his face and I never once heard him raise his voice in anger. Though he would attend drinking parties, he never touched alcohol. Nevertheless, he invariably chatted and laughed with us all night long. He also never smoked.
>
> Regarding his Karate, my strongest memory is of his Tsuki. It seemed to suddenly slip forward out of nowhere, and I was never able to figure out how to block it.
>
> This was strange because his Tsuki seemed to be slow, despite that fact that it was fast. Invariably, his Tsuki found its way past my defenses as I was unable to block it either from above or below. Truly a marvelous strike.
>
> Looking back, I often wonder if he had not passed away at such a young age, just in his thirties, how deep into the mysteries of Karate would he have delved? What aspects would he have perfected and what could he have taught us?

-Egami Shigeru

Following, Shimoda Sensei's sudden death, Funakoshi Gigo was asked to take over as the Karate Shihan at Takushoku University and Waseda University.

Students from both universities entreated Gigo,

You have already become the Elder Sensei's right-hand man, we wish for you to become the Karate Shihan.

To which Gigo replied,

I have nowhere near the capacity to take on that role.

However, though he refused the position twice, in the end, after the third request, he was beaten by his opponent's persistence and relented.

-Kaku Kozo

Former Shotokan Head Instructor Takagi Jotaro Shotokan discussed the transition from Shimoda Sensei to Gigo Sensei.

When Shimoda Sensei, passed away suddenly Gigo Sensei took his place. He assisted Gichin Sensei, kept a dialogue with the Kotei, Senior Students, put up his own money for the construction of the Shotokan Dojo, and overall became the core of the organization.

-Takagi Jotaro Shotokan Head Instructor
Record of Memories of Egami Shigeru 江上茂追想録
By Okura Jiro 大倉二郎 1981

So, in 1935 Gigo Sensei became the official instructor for Waseda University. That same year he started a Karate club at his home and also took the Waseda Karate club to Kansai and Kyushu for demonstrations. They left on July 21st and went to first Nagoya and then Kobe doing demonstrations, before doing a demonstration at Wakamatsu City Junior High School in northern Kyushu. Around this time, Gigo was frequently heard to say, *The way my father does Karate is no good.*

In all likelihood this was referring to how Gichin Sensei had, by this point, become comfortable as an older person and this was reflected in his Karatedo demonstrations. In other words, Gigo wanted to focus on practical applications of the art. Further, while *Ateru Karate*, full-contact Karate, was banned at the time, he was envisioning eventually moving towards a free-form Kumite format that would basically be a *Shiai*, duel.

-Kaku Kozo

That same year, on May 25th Funakoshi Gichin published *Karatedo Kyohan*, switching the Kanji used for Karate from "Chinese Hand" to "Empty Hand." Karate was at last able to reach a general market. Calligrapher and Karate practitioner Uemura Tsunejiro (1906~2002) recalled that *Karatedo Kyohan* sold quickly, a fact he confirmed when he walked around the famous bookstore area of Jimbocho.

> *Karatedo Kyohan* was being very well received, copies were flying off the shelves. I quite enjoyed walking around the bookstores in Jimbocho and seeing our *Karatedo Kyohan* book lined up on the shelves with all the other titles.

> -Uemura Tsunejiro
> *Recollections of the Shotokan and Karatedo Kyohan*

During the war, *Karatedo Kyohan* went out of print but was republished in May of Showa 60 (1985.) Uemura recalls encountering the book again after nearly half a century,

> It was like seeing again what everyone was like fifty years ago, I felt overjoyed, like I had just been reunited with a deceased child.

> -Uemura Tsunejiro

The road to building a dedicated Dojo was long, and from 1922~1939 various facilities were used. The first was simply one room at the Meisho Juku, a dormitory for students from Okinawa. Meisho Juku was a dormitory built specifically for students from Okinawa studying in Tokyo. According to Gima Shinkin,

> The plans were finalized in March of 1912, which was the 45th year of the Meiji Emperor. However, his royal highness passed away on July 13th meaning the first year of the Taisho Emperor began on that day. As construction was completed in September of that year, the dormitory was called Meisho 明正, taking the first Kanji of Meiji 明治 and the second Kanji of Taisho 大正.
> It was a wooden two-story building with twelve rooms for 24~25 students and a twenty mat lecture hall/gathering space.

Near the Meisho Juku there were many residences with shops underneath. Five or six of the younger shop staff, railroad employees and post office workers came and took some lessons, but they didn't last long.
Fujiwara
I asked Konishi and he told me that on a typical weekday there would be five or six students with thirteen or fourteen on the weekends. The fee differed, some people paid 20 Sen, some paid 50 Sen.

-Gima Shinkin
近代空手道の歴史を語る：対談
A Conversation about the History of Modern Karatedo
1986

A room at the Meisho Juku dormitory was used as a Dojo from around 1922~1927 before training transferred to the Yushinkan Dojo in Hongo Masago. This was often referred to as the "Masago-cho Dojo."

Eventually the organization found a small house to rent in Yumicho Town, however they also continued to use the Yushinkan Dojo in Masagocho. The Meisho Juku dormitory was also sometimes used for demonstrations. On November 8th of 1928 a demonstration was held for the former Sumo Yokozuna Onishikiseki. Gigo Sensei also began teaching two sessions starting in 1930, focusing on Kumite.

In 1931 they were no longer able to use the Yushinkan Dojo and they trained primarily at the Masago Dojo, however later evening training re-started at the Yushinkan Dojo, but this ended again in late 1932. Eventually, the Shotokan Dojo was completed in 1939

Picture of (from left to right) Uemura Tsunejiro, Hayashi Yoshiaki and Funakoshi Gigo in front of the Shotokan Dojo sign board they carved.

Shotokan by Uemura Tsunejiro done in the same style showing what the whole sign would have looked like. (1938)

Shoto was Gichin Sensei's Gago, artist name. When we were moving the Dojo from Masagocho to the new Dojo, Gigo Sensei wanted a new sign for the entrance. It was Gigo Sensei's idea to use Gichin Sensei's artist name and call the Dojo Shotokan.

We got a fantastic piece of wood about three feet wide and two feet tall. So, after Gigo Sensei decided on Shotokan, we decided the style of calligraphy and I set about doing dozens of drafts until I finally got one that well suited the horizontal and vertical dimensions of the board. The final style for the Shotokan board was Shoten, an ancient style of writing Kanji often used on official seals.

We realized if we hired sign board shop to carve it for us, it would be prohibitively expensive. So, Hayashi Yoshiaki suggested we try carving it ourselves. The three of us, Gigo Sensei, Hayashi and myself, thought it was a fine idea and we all set to work. Though we knew in principle about carving a sign board, we were all amateurs and the tools we had were small knives suitable for more intricate work than what was required, so it was slow going. Our plan was for each of us to carve one Kanji, however the grain of the wood was very hard and the tips of our blades snapped off. With our progress coming to a standstill, we cleaned up the Kanji as best we could, colored the Kanji with paint and hung it in front of the entrance. In the end the sign with Shotokan written horizontally, that everyone strolled under on their way into the Dojo, was a beautiful piece of amateur workmanship.

-Uemura Tsunejiro

Uemura Wado also conducted calligraphy lessons following the afternoon training session, noting that there were so many people seeking to join the lessons that there weren't enough desks. Gigo Funakoshi Sensei was also a longtime student.

Since it was immediately after training, everyone's hands were shaking a bit and the calligraphy was quite poor. However, after recovering everyone did better, provided we stuck with large Kanji.

-Uemura Tsunejiro

Uemura Wado, who was a blackbelt, also noted that some curious characters showed up at the Shotokan Dojo, recalling a time when Gigo Sensei saw the name "Sagoya Tomeo" in the Dojo logbook.

Gigo Sensei turned to me and asked,
Is this the Sagoya from that incident?
I replied,
It is.
Gigo Sensei asked,
Does he train seriously?
I replied
He does. He is the first one to clean the floors with a Zokin rag in the morning, he is respectful to others and follows the Dojo rules. At first, he was a little rough during training and I thought about asking him to quit, however I don't think that's necessary for now let's just see how he does.

-Uemura Tsunejiro

Sagoya Tomeo immediately after his attempted assassination of the prime minister. The woven grass cap being placed over his head was commonly used to protect the identity of suspects.
Osaka Asahi Newspaper Special Edition November 17th, 1930

Diagram of the Assassination Attempt on Prime Minister Hamaguchi Osachi 1930

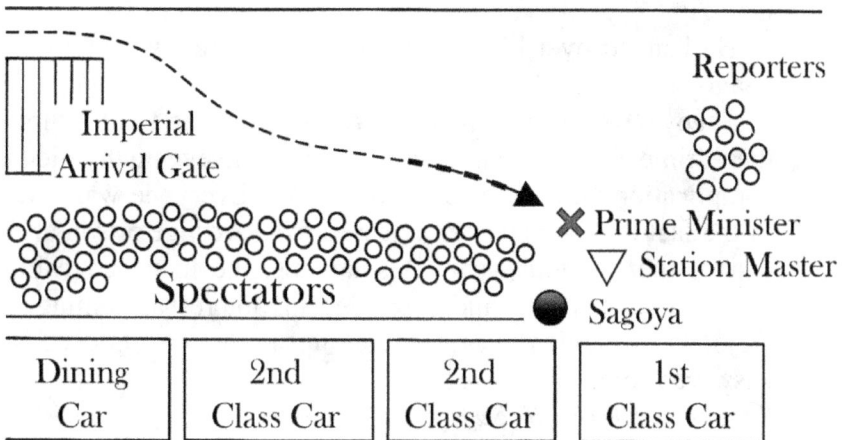

Illustration showing how Sagoya attempted his assassination of the prime minister. He used a German made Mauser C96 pistol.

This was apparently the same Sagoya that attempted to assassinate Prime Minister Hamaguchi by shooting him as he tried to board a train inside Tokyo Station on November 14th 1930. It was virtually the same spot where Prime Minister Hara Takashi was assassinated nine years earlier. The gunshot did not immediately prove fatal but Hamaguchi died from a related infection five months later.

Sagoya and his accomplices were tried and, in 1932, Sagoya was sentenced to death for attempted murder. However, his death sentence was reduced to life in prison and was released from prison in 1940 as part of a general amnesty for those who took part in politically motivated murders. Sagoya died in 1972. It seems likely this episode occurred after he was released from prison. Shotokan member Togawa Yukio actually wrote about the episode in his book *Assassin: The History of Assassination in Modern Japan* and included his recollections of the man.

It was spring of Showa 16 (1940) if I recall correctly. A man came to the Shotokan Karate Dojo in Toyoshima Ward, Mejiro. He was a brawny fellow, a little short and little fat.

We were in the middle of morning training and a student went to the door to meet him. The man spoke in a gravelly voice, I am interested in learning Karate, so I would like to join your Dojo.

He handed over his card which was printed with the name "Sagoya Tomeo."

Sagoya Tomeo was the name of the man who fired a shot at then Prime Minister Hamaguchi Yukio, who eventually died of complications from the assassin's bullet. Everyone was aware of the fact that he had been released from Kosuge prison at the end of the previous year. Despite this, the man had calmly handed over his card and expressed his interest in joining the Dojo, so the student was suddenly unsure how to proceed and answered somewhat vaguely,

So, you are THE Mr. Sagoya…so then…

Yes, that is me, Sagoya.

The student simply blinked at this straightforward answer. Typically, any person that asks to join would be accepted straightaway, but faced with a person with that kind of history, a senior member took over, and said simply,

We will let you know tomorrow…
And with that Sagoya went home.

After morning training finished I was wiping the sweat off my body when I heard the Shihan calling me. At the time I was a manager at the Dojo, albeit the low man on the totem pole. Heading to the back of the Dojo, all the managers were present including Shihan Funakoshi Gichin, who wrote his name Fu 浮 na 名 koshi 腰 (he has since changed the Kanji to Funa 船 Koshi 越) as well as assistant Shihan Gigo (Gichin's second son, now deceased.)[3] It goes without saying we were meeting to decide whether or not to allow Sagoya to join the Dojo.

We shouldn't be near a dangerous person like that.
People will begin to think our Dojo leans to the right.

These and other such opinions were offered.

-Togawa Yukio

Apparently, there were also those that felt he had served his time. At one point, despite his low position, Togawa was asked for his opinion on the matter.

I always felt that time moved forward and it wasn't good to dwell upon the past. The man had faced the possibility of his own execution and come to terms with it and now he was trying to restart his life by doing intensive training. So, in my opinion it's best not to slam the door shut on his nose race he's trying to do that so in short, I argued in favor of allowing him to join the Dojo. At that point Gigo Sensei agreed with me.

I feel the same way. I am in favor of judging the person as he is and not picking apart every part of his life. It seems clear that the man that took part in the assassination and the man that came out of that hellhole of a prison are of a completely different mindset.

-Togawa Yukio

---

[3] The brackets are by the author. He refers to Funakoshi Gigo as Gichin's "second son."

In the end, Sagoya joined the Dojo though the members were cautioned not to try and pry open his old wounds. Regarding his Karate ability, Togawa was not particularly impressed and thought that his extensive Judo training made his Karate style somewhat unusual.

I never thought his Karate was particularly good. As a very adept Judo practitioner, his movements were heavy and he almost seemed to be moving in slow motion. That being said, he was very passionate about training. He wasn't one of those people who wanted to get good quick, or attain a Dan rank as soon as possible, rather I saw that he was dedicating himself wholly to using Karate to reforge himself. Shihan Gigo would frequently comment to us,

Sagoya's Karate is different from what you all are doing. His style of Karate is one not concerned with becoming technically proficient or powerful. That being said, his Tsuki is quite tricky to block.

I was in total agreement with that sentiment; his Tsuki was like a blunt instrument that came barreling at you and was therefore hard to block. While his technique hardly consisted of nimble movement and changes, he had a powerful strike that would invariably find its target. Curiously his somewhat reckless style of training meant that he slowly edged ahead of other practitioners that began around the same period.
Gigo Sensei, watching Sagoya train commented,

He is the type of guy who, if he is moving in a positive direction he will end up better, however if he falls in with a bad crowd, he will get progressively more evil.

Gigo Sensei passed away soon after the war ended, but he always kept an eye on the man named Sagoya Tomeo.

-Togawa Yukio
Assassin: The History of Assassination in Modern Japan
暗殺者：近代日本暗殺史
1958

Uemura Tsunejiro also commented on Sagoya's Karate technique.

Sagoya was a bit short and on the fat side but he was quick to respond. His technique was a little clumsy but he was passionate. After about a year he became a Yudansha, black belt or higher, but one day he appeared and announced,
I have to go serve in Manshu.
After the war I heard he was involved in right wing youth groups in the Ikebukuro area, but I never met him again, except for seeing his face in line to pay his respects at Funakoshi Gichin's funeral.

-Uemura Tsunejiro

In Showa 14 (1939) Shotokan Dojo was completed in Toyoshima Ward, Zoshigaya and Gigo Sensei became the vice president. Shotokan Head Instructor Takagi Jotaro and Egami Shigeru both commented on the significance of the new Dojo.

In 1929 Funakoshi Gichin changed the name of his art from Karate Jutsu to Karatedo. Changing the name from Karate Jutsu to Karatedo was a bold decision by Funakoshi Gichin Sensei, it can be thought of as the day Karatedo began and it is the reason Karatedo began to spread throughout Japan. I would say that this is the first pivotal moment in Karate.

Initially, morning training was conducted by Gichin Sensei while evening training was done by Gigo Sensei. This is the era when the foundations of what would be, in later times, seen as the powerful and applicable in real life Shotokan Karate. This is the second pivotal time in Shotokan Karate.

I am not sure people are aware that during the war, the Shotokan was considered to be one of the great Dojo in the imperial capital, after the Judo Kodokan and the Kendo Nakayama Hakudo Yurinkan Dojo.

-Takagi Jotaro Shotokan Head Instructor

Managing the Dojo was extremely difficult for Gigo Sensei and he often covered any losses with his own salary...That being said, that was the state of affairs and he never complained about it. Rather he was solely focused on doing whatever was necessary to expand this art.

Once, when Gigo Sensei was explaining a technique, I served as his Uke, and in the process got thoroughly thrashed. Gigo Sensei talked about how, in real life, techniques don't end at a predetermined point, rather a duel will move away from what a Kata dictates. Saying this the demonstration continued until I was complexly and utterly beaten down. That experience of doing a demonstration with that level of intensity is thoroughly ingrained into every fiber of my being.

Afterward, he came up to me and said with a big smile on his face, *Suman Suman*, "Sorry, that was a tough demonstration!"

That was the kind of Sensei he was.

-Egami Shigeru

Hironishi Motonobu (1913~1999,) former President of the Japan Karatedo Shotokan Society was able to ask both Gichin Sensei and Gigo Sensei about technical aspects regarding techniques.

Heian Yondan no Yoko Geri

In Heian Yondan there are two Yoko Geri, one with your right foot and one with your left foot. The Yoko Geri in Heian Yondan was, up until the eighth or ninth year of Showa, a side facing Mae Geri.

Gigo Sensei told us to do a Yoko Geri when training Heian Yondan, so we followed his instructions. However, when considering the flow of the Kata, something felt slightly off. It felt like the flow was being interrupted. On the other hand, I felt no sense something is off when doing a side kick with my right foot in Heian Nidan. This is no doubt because before the Yoko Geri, you slide your left foot, which is behind you, a half step towards your right.

However, when you do a side kick with your right foot in Heian Yondan, I always found my breathing would stop for a moment, no matter how much I worked at it. This mean I felt the flow of the movement would also pause. I asked Gichin Sensei about this and this is what he told me.

You are exactly right. However, the purpose of training in this way is to focus on the Yoko Geri rather than the flow of the kata. So please continue with that important point in mind. Learning how to turn to the side and do a Mae Geri does not require very much practice before you can reach an acceptable level. The essence of this training is to focus on the much more difficult Yoko Geri. With sufficient training that Iwakan, sense something is off, will gradually disappear.

In Showa 16 (1941) I went to Tokyo and when I saw the Karate training being done at universities, I realized they were all doing Yoko Geri. I didn't detect any Iwakan in the students.

Nowadays, all the standard kata use side kicks. Further, other schools of Karate besides the Shotokan have adopted the Yoko Geri. I think this is a big achievement by Gigo Sensei.

-Hironishi Motonobu

Showa 15 (1940)

In March of that year Gigo starts Karatedo Club at Chuo University and becomes head instructor.

In May, Gichin Sensei and Gigo Sensei do a demonstration in Kyoto along with other Shotokan members.

December 8th 1941

Japan enters the Second World War.

April 29th, Showa 20 (1945)

Shotokan Dojo is destroyed by allied bombs

> Just as the Americans were making land in the Philippines, my second tour in the army as a reporter ended. I returned home around the time Okinawa fell. As soon as I got home, I went to the Shotokan Dojo and found nothing but a pile of ashes. In short order, the war ended.
>
> There was no Dojo, the students I had taught were scattered and I didn't know where they were. Everything was a mass of confusion.
>
> -Togawa Yukio (1912~2004)
> *Memories of the Shotokan*

August 15th Showa 20 (1945)

Japan Surrenders

> In this crucial period where everything was coming together, the Pacific War suddenly stopped any further progress and Gigo Sensei was never granted a full opportunity to demonstrate his vision.
>
> -Kaku Kozo 加来耕三

> After long searching I finally found Gigo Sensei in the half-burned apartment in Meijiro. He was lying on the floor half-dead. Hironishi and I frequently tended to him.
> Gigo Sensei moaned,
> *Maybe if there was some penicillin...*
> I set about wildly trying to locate some penicillin, even going so far as to use my connections to the newspaper to get through

to the occupying forces. Finally, I got hold of one vial of penicillin and took it to Gigo's bedside, but I was too late.
Gigo held the penicillin weakly in his hand and said,
So this is penicillin...

After Gigo Sensei passed away I didn't meet any Dojo members for some time. However, several months later I randomly ran into Hironishi at the black market in front of Shinbashi Station. His clothes were a mess and he was looking like a vagabond but he called out to me with his usual infectious voice *Yo!* We shared a glass each of Kasutori Shochu, low quality moonshine, and a plate of 5 Yen stewed squid. As we ate Hironishi said,

I realized eh, I can't just let my passion for Karate be extinguished. You know what I'm saying, I'm gonna keep going. The Americans yeah, they are talking about taking Budo away from Japanese people. We aren't gonna let that happen. It wouldn't be fair to Sensei, considering all he's done.

-Togawa Yukio (1912~2004)
Memories of the Shotokan

Funakoshi Gigo died on November 24th at the age of thirty-nine.

In my opinion, Elder Teacher Shoto Sensei, Shimoda Sensei and Gigo Sensei were all able to completely overcome the physical conditions that afflicted all three of them, namely: being short, being of slight build and suffering from an illness. Through diligent practice, they refined and expanded Karatedo as a martial art and, over endless days and nights, strove to perfect it.

Both Shimoda Sensei and Gigo Sensei burned through their physical strength and passed from this mortal coil while they were still in the midst of following their path. This left the Elder Teacher to continue to forge and mold his students. When he was in his eighties he commented to me,

I feel like I have only just now begun to have a true understanding of Jodan Uke.

-Egami Shigeru

How the New Dojo Was Developed
By Funakoshi Gigo
January 29th 1939

How the New Dojo Was Developed
By Funakoshi Gigo

January 29th of the fourteenth year of Showa (1939.) This is a day Karatedo practitioners have long waited for, the inauguration ceremony for the All Japan Karatedo Shotokan Dojo. I would like to express my thanks and my deepest appreciation to those who worked tirelessly to achieve this goal, including to those who planned and designed the Dojo, the Shotokan management and students as well as all those who, through their deep understanding of Karatedo, offered critical support.

Looking back to spring eighteen years ago, my father, who was working as part of the Okinawa Prefectural school affairs division had travelled to Tokyo for the fist time to introduce Karate at the First National Athletic Exhibition in Tokyo organized by the Ministry of Education. Following the exhibition, he was planning on returning home, however he was urged by Kosugi Hoan Sensei[4] to borrow the lecture hall of the Meisho Juku dormitory near Koishikawa Suidobashi[5] That hall became the first place where a Karatedo instructor could hang up a sign offering lessons.

The Meisho Juku was a dormitory for students from Okinawa Prefecture. Initially many of the dormitory students thought the whole enterprise was very interesting and even trained with the Karate students. However, as the number of Karate students increased, we gradually began to get complaints from the university students about the noise, specifically that they found it hard to concentrate on their studies. Thus I, and my father as well, got in the habit of cautioning students lower their power level when teaching so there wasn't so much noise.

In this fashion, we continued daily training, but in a somewhat unsatisfactory manner, which made us realize we needed to build our own separate Dojo. That being said we couldn't do anything without money.

As my father was fond of saying in between training sessions, "You know the saying, *If you endure sitting atop a stone for three years,*

---

[4] Kosugi Hoan 小杉放庵(1881~ 1964)
[5] Modern day Kasuga, Bunkyo Ward, Tokyo

you can succeed at any venture. [6] As it had been four or five years since I came to Tokyo, I believe I would like to build a Dojo." Frankly, at that time training was mentally taxing.

With that in mind around the second year of Showa (1927) elder Senpai[7] from Okinawa Prefecture as well as Karate students started a group to examine the feasibility of building a Karatedo Dojo. We initially tapped Okinawa Prefecture Senpai Rear Admiral Kanna [8] to head the Karate support committee and we even began planning construction, however our timing was bad and, in the end, while choking back tears, we had to abandon the project. For some time after that we continued to hold rather restrained training in the lecture hall in the dormitory, all the while university after university was starting up Karate training clubs.

Finally in the spring of the sixth year of Showa (1931,) we became unable to use the Meisho Juku dormitory as a Dojo anymore. My father was very troubled but fortunately Nakayama Hakudo Sensei[9] was kind enough to lend us use of his Yushinkan Dojo in the evenings after 7pm. Meanwhile the Karate clubs at other universities were expanding rapidly and amongst them many were concerned about the issue of building a Honbu Dojo, main training center.

Mr. Noguchi, who was head of the Waseda University Karate Club at the time, gathered the heads of other Karate clubs such as Mr. Matsumoto at Takushoku University, Mr. Nakamura at Keio University and others, and the students embarked on a great discussion of the problem. This large group of students were serious in their determination to address the problem of building a Honbu Dojo, however the fact was they were students, and the meetings were

---

[6] This is a variation of the common expression *Ishi no Ue nimo San Nen* 石の上にも三年 perseverance prevails/three years on a cold stone will make the stone warm

[7] Japanese word referring to your senior. Any person older than you in an organization. This is referring to a Senpai of Funakoshi Gigo.

[8] Kanna Kenwa 漢那憲和 (1877~1950)

[9] Nakayama Hakudo 中山博道 (1872 ~ 1958) a martial artist active in sword and pole arts. Coined the term, *Karate was Sude ni yoru Kenjutsu de Aru* 唐手は素手による剣術である
Kenjutsu without a sword is Karate or *Karate is when you do Kenjutsu barehanded.*

unable to produce any tangible results. I must say I bow my head in respect to the effort those students put forth. In the end, until an opportunity to build a Honbu Dojo presented itself, we put all our energy into travelling around and conducting seminars.

The topic of "Where is the Honbu Dojo?" did not just come up when the heads of university Karate clubs met, but also whenever a group of students got together, and we frequently heard how troubled everyone was concerning this issue. I would get depressed every time a passionate student would bring up this topic and really felt the weight of the responsibility I bore.

In response we considered building a hut, kind of like a barracks, despite feeling that such a structure would hardly do justice to our students or our art. As we pondered various other plans, it came to our attention that there was a house for rent in the Yumicho section of Tokyo with a sizeable garden.[10]

So, we set about cutting down all the trees and laid down a wooden floor that was about eighteen Tatami mats, 320 square feet, in size. With our new *Noten Dojo*, outdoor training space, our students were finally free to practice uninhibited. That being said, the weather did not always favor us while we trained at our outdoor Dojo and we sometimes had to unfortunately cancel training due to rain or snow. This meant when we woke up every morning, we were concerned what the weather would be. If rain began to fall after we started training, we would carry on despite the people slipped and tumbled. However, as everyone was passionate about training no one complained, and we pushed on.

Of course, there were times when we had no choice but to stop training, which meant everyone began chatting, with some students making serious proposals,

---

[10] This is area, called Bow Field in English, was famous for being the location of many Samurai residences. In relation to Edo Castle the area was to the northeast, meaning it was oriented towards Kimon, the Devil's Gate. This is an unlucky direction since devils can enter the castle from that direction. Thus, as protection, a great archery field was built in order to ward off bad luck, thus the name Yumicho, Bow Field. Later, after the Toeizan Kanei-ji Temple was built to protect the Kimon approach to Edo Castle, the bow field was moved elsewhere, but the name of the town remained.

Sensei we can each contribute one roof tile or one log for a column, please build a Dojo with a roof so that we can train every day!

Every time we heard something like this, we felt kind of powerless and were overcome with emotion that we couldn't adequately respond with action.

We decided to try to find a place to build a Dojo and ran ads in the newspaper two or three times, "Seeking a house with a big garden to rent" however trying to find a cheap house to rent that had a large garden was a lost cause in central Tokyo. Whenever the Shotokan board of governors met, even if the topic of building a Dojo was put forward as an item on the agenda, it was invariably passed over as being not the appropriate time.

In March of Showa 12 (1937) I had to visit Torii Sensei in Ueno. As it turned out Dr. Aikawa, an instructor at the Imperial Medical University, was also there and when I humbly brought up the issue of building a Dojo with the two Sensei, they replied,

We will offer our assistance, so you should probably hurry up and gather any other donations.

Thus, on their advice I quickly sprang into action and upon returning home discussed the news with my father. He was delighted and surprised that the two Sensei had concerned themselves with the construction of a Dojo and began planning immediately. The next day on his way back from work he picked up the Dojo visitor's book,[11] and stated that this time he was determined to make the new Dojo a reality. On his way home my father happened to run into executive secretary Uemura,[12] and he told him about the meeting with the two Sensei in Ueno. Uemura replied positively,

This is our chance to bring our plan to reality!

He had Uemura use his masterful calligraphy to write a letter that outlined the plan to build a Dojo. Combining the letter with the visitor's book, my father departed to consult with Aikawa Sensei. The

---

[11] This appears to be a book of members or supporters who have committed to donating to a new Dojo.

[12] Calligrapher Uemura Tsunejiro 植村常次郎 (1906 ~ 2002.)

doctor was delighted that things were proceeding quickly, and he encouraged Dr. Saito, a professor and the Japanese Medical University, to support the endeavor and Dr. Saito quickly agreed to support the project, further spurring our motivation.

The three of them then called for Torii Sensei,

I agree to the plan you have crafted, let us carry it out!

And Torii Sensei, when presented with the Dojo visitor's book, gladly signed his name and added,

I am praying for the success of this project.

Needless to say, we were all overjoyed. It goes without saying that if things had proceeded in this fashion from the outset, we would have made the Dojo a reality long ago.

I made my way to the orthopedic surgery department at the Imperial Japanese Hospital, a place that we frequented, and made the donation pledge book available. Despite being in the middle of work, the doctors all immediately agreed with our proposal and signed their names while enthusiastically wishing for the project to succeed.

In short order we held a committee meeting where we requested the members all approve the plan to build a new Dojo, and all committee members immediately agreed. We then set about discussing how we would gather and handle donations, and with that, in June of Showa 12 (1937) the Committee to Construct the All Japan Karatedo Honbu was born.

However, as the saying goes *Sunzen-Shakuma*, while there is good fortune to be had in this world, there are many demons running about causing bad fortune.[13] Almost as soon as we began taking concrete steps to make the plan into fruition, the Second Sino-Japanese War began and many of those who had agreed to support the construction were, one after the other, drafted into the military, meaning at one point the whole project collapsed.[14]

---

[13] *Sunzen Shakuma*寸善尺魔 The final Kanji魔 meaning devil, probably is not referring abstractly to evil but to a monster that acts to prevent humans from becoming happy.

[14] The Second Sino-Japanese War (1937~1945,) began July 7th 1937.

However, his excellency Saigo Yoshinosuke[15] (1906~1997) who was the president of the All Japan Student Karatedo Association, offered the following words of strong encouragement,

Considering the current situation in the world, I feel it is imperative that the citizens on the home front improve their physical fitness, thus your plans should proceed.

This served to infuse the committee members with new energy, and that new motivation eventually led to real success. On August 3rd of Showa 13 (1938) Zoshigaya was selected as the location and construction was set to start on August 23rd with a completion date of around mid-October. However, due to unprecedented bad weather, construction was repeatedly delayed, with the actual start of construction not occurring until mid-November.

So, after enduring one thing after another for more than a decade, struggling to introduce Karatedo while training in a temporary Dojo and having one plan after another fall through, we had finally reached this point. It was thanks to our conversations with Torii Sensei, Saito Sensei and Aikawa Sensei, that the project to construct a Dojo was set into motion. Though these three Sensei do not have any direct experience training Karate, they nevertheless have a thorough understanding of the essence of Karate. And on this day where we celebrate the completion of the All Japan Karatedo Shotokan Dojo I offer my sincerest thanks to these three Sensei, who served as the impetus to begin construction.

His excellency Saigo who offered his advice to the construction committee, as well as the many Sensei who helped us to surmount the numerous difficulties that faced. I would also like to express my deepest gratitude to the Karate committee members, without whose effort the construction of the Dojo would have been impossible.

Finally I would like to express my appreciation to Ohama Nobu[16] President of the Waseda University Karate Club and founder of the Funakoshi Gichin Karate Support Committee, as well as to offer my

---

[15] Saigo Yoshinosuke 西郷吉之助 (1906~1997) was the grandson of Saigo Takamori. Most high-ranking government officials were referred to with the honorific "his excellency.".

[16] Ohama Nobumoto 大濱信泉 (1891~1976)

sincerest gratitude to General Secretaries Kugimiya Yukio [17] and Akimoto Norio[18] who ground their bones to powder negotiating the final location.[19]

Funakoshi Gigo
January 29th 1939

---

[17] Kugimiya Yukio 釘宮幸雄 (?~?)

[18] Akimoto Norio 秋元則雄 (?~?)

[19] The cost of the Shotokan Dojo at that time was about ¥15,000. In 1939 ¥1 was worth about ¥1,800 today so a total of ¥27,480,000 or about $186,000 in today's money.

Karate to Wa?
What is Karate?
Part 1
Funakoshi Gigo

Taiso 体操 **Exercise Magazine**
Volume 9, April 1939

空手道とは （一）

富名腰義豪

けませんから、型の順序を知る前に、一應基本練習の内、中段直突、下段拂受、上段受、中段手刀受の四種を二、三日程實際に練習したならば、初段の順序を憶えるには便利であります。

に開いて八字立になり、左右の拳を握り締めながら、肘を伸して兩脇下に下げ、頸を引き、胸を張り、眼は正面を見、自然體で、丹田に力を入れます。この用意の體勢は、そこから敵に攻撃を受けても、自由に防禦し、敵を制する心構へでなければなりません。用意の體勢も亦型の一部分でありますから、修練を積んだ人と初步の人とでは立ち方に於て既に初型の一部分が異ってゐます。この構へ方を見ますと、その人の次に展開する型の演武の大體を豫想する事が出來ますから、用意の構へから眞劍に練習する様にして下さい。

第二圖

第一線平安初段用意の姿勢

平安初段

平安は初段から五段までありまして、初段の型を分解しますと、次の五種類の手の働きと四種類の足取から成立つてゐます。

手 — 中段直突、上段打落
　　下段拂受、中段手刀受

足 — 前屈立、レの字立、後屈立

以上の様に型の各々の動作は殆んど基本練習のとろで練習したものでありまして、わずかに中段打落だけが新しく加はつたのみであります。これも基本練習を修得した者には左程困難なものではあ

第一圖

體の仕方

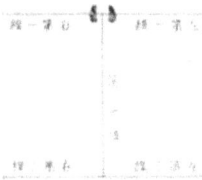

平安初段は以上の働きを組合せたものでありまして、演武編は大體「エ」字型で、二十一擧動か揚なり、時間も約四十秒から五十秒程度で終ります。

（禮）型の前後には必ず禮をします。禮も型の一部分でありまして、演武する前に適當な位置を定め閉足立になり兩手を自然に前に垂れ、上體を

し前に屈して第一圖の様に行ひます。

第三圖　平安段初（二）

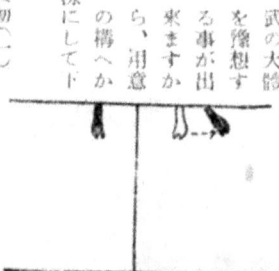

ら眞劍に練習する様にして下さい。

Dai Ichi Zu

Rei no Shikata
How to bow properly

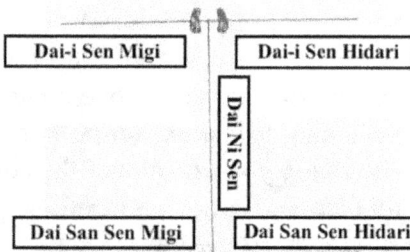

Dai-i Sen Migi		Dai-i Sen Hidari
	Dai Ni Sen	
Dai San Sen Migi		Dai San Sen Hidari

Dai Ichi Zu
First Picture

Heian Shodan

There are Heian Kata from Shodan to Godan. If we analyze the Shodan Kata we find it is comprised of five kinds of hand movements and four types of foot and leg movements.

Hands – Chudan Choku Zuki Jodan Uchi Otoshi Gedan Harai Uke Chudan Shuto Uke	Feet – Zenkutsu Dachi Standing like レ Kokutsu Dachi

As you can see the Kata is comprised entirely of the fundamental movements done in practice. That being said, the addition of Chudan Uchi Otoshi is new, albeit a small change. Anyone who has done *Kihon Renshu*, Fundamental Training, is unlikely to have any difficulty with this technique. Thus, before studying the steps of this Kata, you should go out and practice the following four parts of the Kihon Renshu for two or three days:

- Choku Zuki
- Gedan Harai Uke
- Jodan Uke
- Chudan Shuto Uke

This will be very beneficial to learning the order of the Shodan Kata. The above description of the movements concludes this introduction to Heian Shodan. When executing this Kata you will do twenty-one actions. The shape you make over the course of this Kata is like the Katakana letter エ and, from start to finish, should take you somewhere between forty and fifty seconds.

Body

You should always do a bow of respect at the beginning and end of the Kata. The Rei, or bow of respect, is also part of the Kata. Before beginning, select an appropriate spot and stand with your feet together and allow your arms to hang down naturally in front of you and bend forward naturally. This is show in Dai Ichi Zu, the first Picture.

Ready position for Heian Shodan
along Dai-i Sen, the first line

第 二 圖 Dai Ni Zu

第一線平安初段用意の姿勢

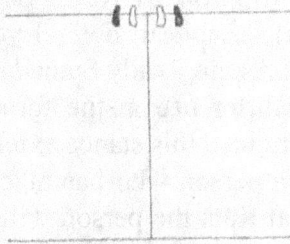

Second Picture

Yoh-I Ready

Having done a bow of respect, you are now standing with your feet together. Go into *Hachimonji Dachi,* standing with your feet like Hachi 八 the Kanji for eight, by first stepping out to the left with your left foot. Then, squeeze both hands into fists while extending your elbows so both fists are hanging below your armpits. Pull your chin in, expand your chest and direct your eyes forward. Once in this *Shizentai,* Natural Body Posture, focus all your power in Tanden, the point just below the navel.

Once you are in this *Yoh-I Shisei,* Ready Stance, if you are attacked by an enemy, you will be able to defend yourself freely and then restrain your opponent. As the Ready Stance is also part of this Kata, there is a discernable difference in the force of presence between practitioners that have trained this stance extensively and beginners.

When you observe a person who has taken this Kamae, you can more or less judge what Kata the person will demonstrate, therefore please train Ready Stance seriously.

（二）平安初段の第二の動作は、左足前の下段拂受から始まりますが、前述の基本練習のところで説明しました様に、先づ顔を左方に向けながら、左拳を右肩、右拳を左腋前に伸ばし、左足を一歩前進させ前腕が房になる様にして、第二圖の様に下段拂受を用意の姿勢から下段拂受をします。此の時、よく目は下を見たり、體を前へ傾けたりし勝ちですから注意して首は眞直ぐ左右を向き、上體を左斜におく様につとめる事が大切であります。

第四圖　平安初段（二）

（三）左下拂受から、左足をそのまゝ、後の右足を一歩踏出しながら、右拳の中段進突をします。上段拂受を通す左拳は、右拳を中段に突き出すと同時に腰に引き付けます。

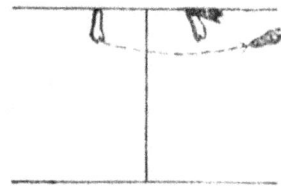

第一線上に、左足をそのまゝ、後の右足を一歩踏出しながら、右拳を左拳前から、左拳を右胸前から、互に交叉して引張る様に反動を付けて、第五圖の

第六圖

第五圖

（三）（二）の場から、右に一百八十度胴轉し、百一線上に引き返しながら、右拳を左拳前から、左拳を右胸前から、互に交叉して引張る様に反動を付けて、第五圖の

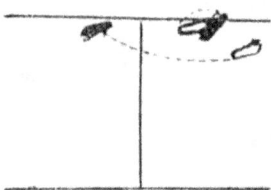

平安初段（三）

第六圖（イ）

如く、前屈右手下段拂受を行ひます。丁度（二）の場合と正反對の位置であります。

第六圖（ロ）

（四）下段拂受をした右手首を敵に掴まれたものと假想して、一歩前に踏み出した右足を半歩引き付けると同時に、右拳を軸にして圖を描く様に過して肩と水平のところに打止めます。圖を描く様に過して打つ意味は、敵が掴んだ手首を、自分の手元にグッと腕を引き寄せた反動で、手槌を上から打つのであります。最初の練習中は大きく腕を過して下さい。

第六圖の（イ）（ロ）は一撃動で行ひます。

（五）敵の手首を打つと同時に、後退して行く

平安初段（四）

第三圖　平安段初（一）

Dai San Zu
Heian Shodan

Dai San Zu
Third Picture

Step One

The first move in Heian Shodan is stepping forward with your left foot forward while doing a Gedan Harai Uke. Specifically, as was previously mentioned in the Kihon Renshu, Fundamental Training, your first move is to turn your face to the left while bringing your left fist up to the height of your right shoulder, while, at the same time extending your right arm so that your right fist in in front of your left arm. Step forward with your left foot into Zenkutsu Dachi. At the same time, uncross your arms as if you are wringing out a towel, ending in a Gedan Harai Uke. This is shown in *Dai San Zu*, the Third Picture.

The transition from Ready Stance to Gedan Harai Uke should be done in one movement, so please practice this thoroughly. When executing the Gedan Harai Uke, a common mistake is allowing your eyes to look down, however doing this will cause you to lose your balance forward, so be sure to turn your face directly left and concentrate on rotating your upper body diagonally to the left. This is important.

第四圖　平安初段（二）

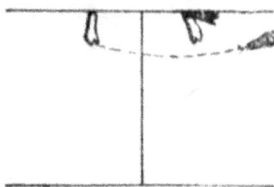

第五圖

（二）安社子の他（？）の運作は、广見前の下
拂受から始りますが、前述の基本練習のところ
で説明しました様に、先づ顏を左方に向けなから
左拳を右肩へ、右拳を左腋前に伸ばし、左足を一
歩前進させ前屈が努になると同時に、交叉してゐ
る両拳を絞る様にして、第三圖の様に下段拂受を
します。用意の姿勢から下段拂受の時、よく目
下を見たり、體が前に倒れたりし勝ちですから
注意して首は頂直ぐ左を向き、上體は左斜におく
様につとめる事が大切であります。

（三）左下拂受から、左
第一線上に、左足をそのま
い、後の右足を一歩踏出
しながら右拳の中段追突を
します。下段拂受をしての
た左拳は、右拳を中段に突
き出すと同時に腰に引き付
けます。

第六圖（イ）

（三）（二）の場合から、右に
左足を軸にして、右に
百八十度廻轉し、五一
線上に引返しなから、
右拳を左拳前から、左
拳を右腋前から、互に
交叉して引張る様に反
動を付けて、第五圖の

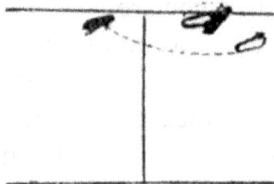

平安初段（三）

第六圖（ロ）

如く、前屈イ子十段拂受を行ひます。上換（？）は
合と正反對の位置であります。

（四）下段拂受をした
右手首を敵に摑まれたも
のと假想して、一步右前
に踏み出した右足を半步
程引付けると同時に、
右拳を軸にして圓を描く
様に力を入れて、手槌で
敵の手首を打つ心持ちで
肩と水平のところに打止めます。圓を描く様に廻
して打つ意味は、敵が摑んだ手首を、自分の手元
にグット腕を引き寄せた返動で、手槌で上から打
つのであります。最初の練習中は大きく腕を廻し
て下さい。

（五）第六圖の（イ）（ロ）は二擧動で行ひます。
敵の手首を打つと同時に、後退して行く
敵をすかさず攻擊する意味で、半步引いた右足を

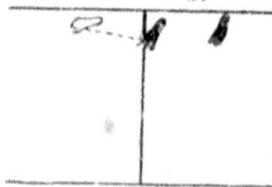

平安初段（四）

Step Two

Fourth Picture

After doing a Gedan Harai Uke with your left fist, bring your right foot forward along *Hidari Dai-i Sen*, the First Line to the Left, while leaving your left foot in place. As you bring your right foot forward from behind, strike Chudan Shintotsu, Mid-Level Advancing Strike, with your right fist.[20] As you strike to Chudan with your right fist, pull your left fist, that just executed a Gedan Harai Uke with, back to your hip.

---

[20] This may be another name for Chudan Choku Zuki.

Step Three

第五圖

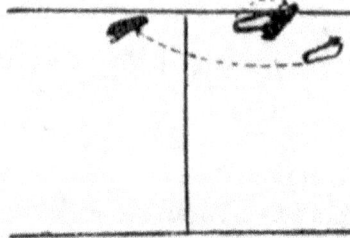

（三）段初安平

Fifth Picture

From your position in Step Two, pivot on your left foot and rotate 180° clockwise, placing your right foot on the *Migi Dai-i Sen*, Right First Line. As you do this bring your right fist across to your left, passing in front of your left fist. Your left fist should be in front of your right arm. Build up tension in both arms as they cross and then strike with a Gedan Harai Uke with your right hand while standing in Zenkutsu. You are now in the exact opposite of the stance shown in Step One.

Step Four

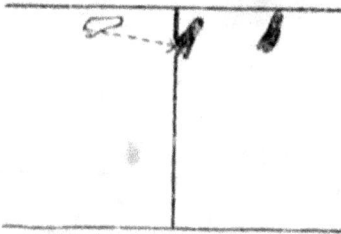

Picture Six (a)   Picture Six (b)

Next, imagine that after you executed a Gedan Harai Uke your opponent then seizes your right wrist. Respond by pulling your right foot, which is out in front, a half step back. At the same time, focus power in your right arm and use it to trace a circle before imagining slamming your *Tezuchi*, Hammer Fist, down on your opponent's wrist. You should end your strike with your right fist level with your shoulder.

The purpose of this technique is to respond to your opponent seizing your wrist. You use Mawashi Uchi, Rotating Hit, to yank your wrist towards yourself before continuing around to strike down with a Hammer Fist on your opponent's wrist, thereby freeing yourself. Initially, please practice making a large circle with your arm.

Pictures Six (a) and Six (b) show the movement.

段に就つて来たものと假定して〈六〉の左下段拂を行ふ。五の左拳追突から、右足を軸にして、左足を第二線上左に九十度廻轉して、左前屈下段受の姿勢になる。

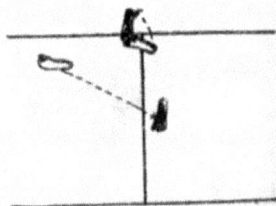

（六）段初安平

そのまゝ軸にして、左足を一歩右一直線上に踏み出すと同時に、圓を描いて打込んだ右拳を引くと共に、腰に構へた左拳を中段突します。

第八圖

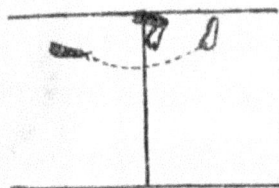

（五）段初安平

（七）下段に拂ひ受した左拳を開いて、七のやうに揚受をする。

第九圖（ロ）

第九圖（イ）

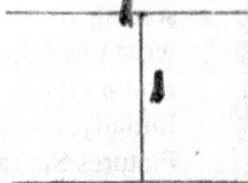

（七）段初安平

（八）次に出てる左足を軸にして、右足を一歩前進する同時に、右手上段揚受をする、この場合〈ロ〉の如く兩手を交叉しながら〈ロ〉をおこなふ。

第十圖（イ）

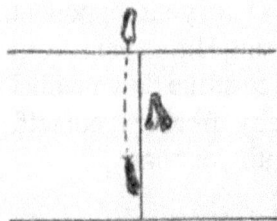

（八）段初安平

Step Five

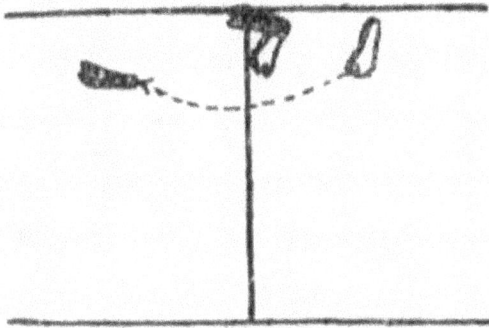

Picture Seven

The moment you strike your opponent's wrist he will withdraw. The moment he drops back you attack by stepping forward with your left foot while pivoting on your right foot, which stays in place. Your left foot should be along the Right Straight Line.

As you step, pull your right fist, which has just traced a circle and struck your opponent's wrist, back to your hip while striking Chudan Tsuki with your left fist.

Step Six

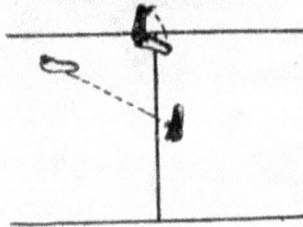

（六）段　初　安　平

Picture Eight

Next, imagine an opponent attacks with a Gedan Keri from your right as you are in the position described in Step Five. Step Six is responding to this with a Hidari Gedan Harai. Focusing your weight on your right foot pivot your body 90°counterclockwise and plant your left foot along Dai Ni Sen, Second Straight Line. As you do this defend against the kick with a Gedan Uke your left fist, which punched directly ahead in Step Five, and end up in left Zenkutsu Dachi.

Step Seven

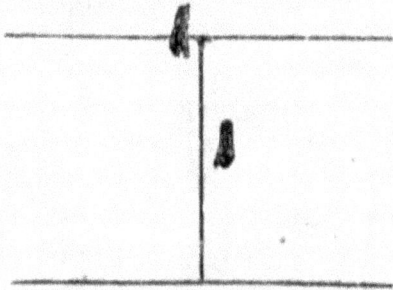

Picture Nine (a)

After completing the Gedan Harai with your left hand, open your hand and raise it in Age Uke as shown in Picture Nine (a.)

Step Eight

（八）段　初　安　平

Picture Nine (b)   Picture Ten (a)

Next, keeping your left foot in place, step forward one step with your right, while lifting your right arm in a Jodan Age Uke. You should end up positioned as shown in Picture Nine (b) and Ten (a.)

段揚受。

第十二圖

（九）段初安平

（九）拳を開き左足を一歩前進して、左拳の上

（十）段初安平

（十）再び同樣に、左拳を開き、右足を一歩進めてから、右拳の揚をする。以上の樣に第二線上に移てから、上段揚受を右二回、左一回と三回續けて行ふのでありますが、最後の右揚受は、腕が顔の上に極る瞬間敵を倒したものと假定して大きな氣合をかけます。

第十三圖

（十二）左足を軸にして右足を一歩前進して中段追突をする。

（十一）左足を軸として左に九十度廻十して前屈左下段拂受の姿勢になる。

平安初段の最後から、右足を軸として左に九十度廻十して前屈左下段拂受の姿勢になる。

（十二）段初安平

（十一）段初安平

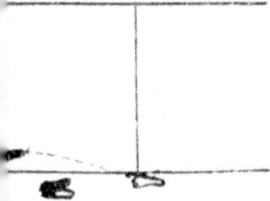

第十四圖

第十五圖

（十三）左足を軸にして、右足を第三線上右に百八十度廻轉し、右拳の下段拂受をする。

（十三）段初安平

Step Nine

第十一圖

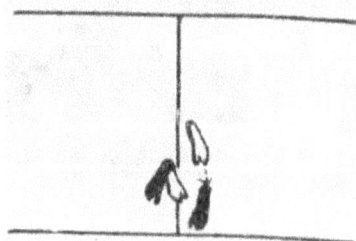

（九）段初安平

Picture Eleven

Relax your fist and step forward with your left foot, while raising your left fist over your head in a Jodan Age Uke. This is shown in Picture Eleven.

Step Ten

Picture Twelve

As you did in the previous step, open your left hand and then step forward with your right foot and raise your right fist in an Age Uke. This ends the movements on the Second Straight Line. After stepping onto this line, you execute two Jodan Age Uke on your right and once on your left for a total of three times in succession.

Note that the final Age Uke will topple the opponent you are envisioning so the moment your arm rises above your face, shout a powerful Kiai.

Step Eleven

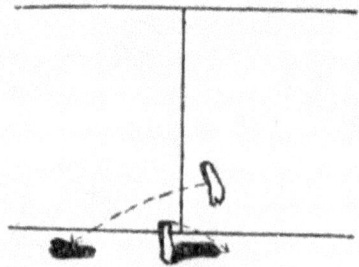

Picture Thirteen

After executing the final Jodan Age Uke with your right hand, step with your left foot 90° out to your right, while pivoting on your right foot. Shift into left Zenkutsu Gedan Harai Uke.

Step Twelve

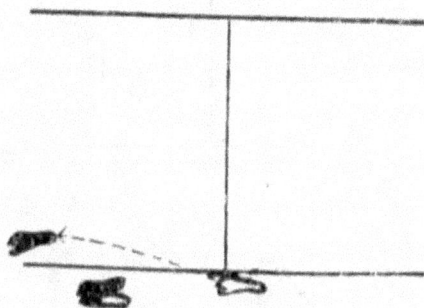

Picture Fourteen

While putting your weight on your left leg, advance with your right foot and strike with Chudan Oizuki.

Step Thirteen

第十五圖

下

（三十）段初安平

Picture Fifteen

Next, put your weight on your left foot and rotate 180°planting your right foot on the Third Straight Line and defend with a right Gedan Harai Uke.

Karate to Wa?
What is Karate?
Part 2
Funakoshi Gigo

Taiso 体操 **Exercise Magazine**
Volume 10, May 1939

空手道とは（二）

富名腰義豪

第十六圖

第十七圖

第十八圖

第十九圖

（十四）左第三線上に、左足を一歩前進させ、中段追突をする。

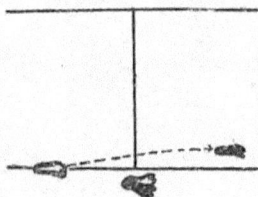

平安初段（十四）

（十五）右足を軸にして、左に左足を第二線上に九十度廻轉し、左拳下段拂受の姿勢になる。

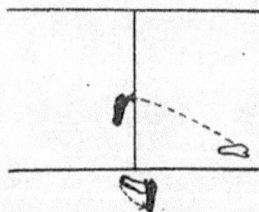

平安初段×（十五）

（十六）右足を第二線上に一歩前進して、中段追突をする。

平安初段（十六）

Step Fourteen

せ、中段追突をする。
に、左足を一歩前進さ
（十四）　左第三線上

第十六圖

（十四）段初安平

Picture Sixteen

Step forward with your left foot along the Third Straight Line and punch with a Chudan Oizuki.

Step Fifteen

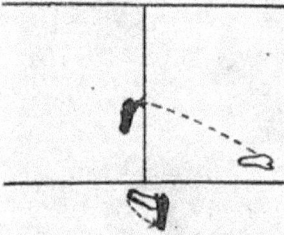

Picture Seventeen

While focusing your weight on your right foot, rotate your body 90° clockwise and place your left foot along the Second Straight Line. Strike with Gedan Harai Uke with your left fist.

Step Sixteen

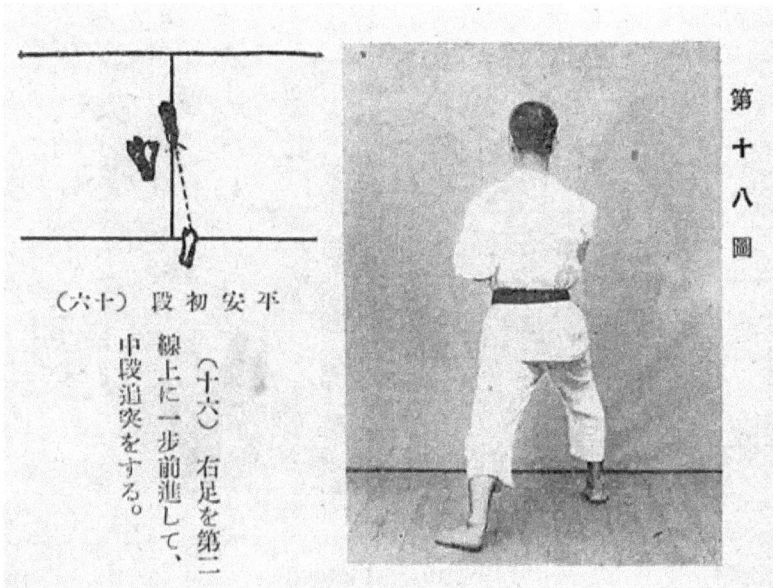

平安初段（十六）

（十六）右足を第二
線上に一歩前進して、
中段追突をする。

第
十
八
圖

Picture Eighteen

Step forward with your right foot onto the Second Straight Line and strike with a Chudan Oizuki.

Step Seventeen

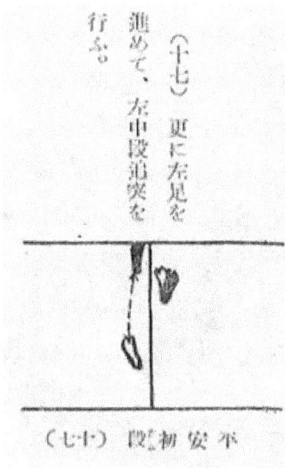

Picture Nineteen

Next, step forward with your left and strike with a Chudan Oizuki with your left fist.

Step Eighteen

再び右足を
進めて、右中段追突し
て、丁度上段揚受に依
つて、前に進んだ第二
線上を、中段追突を三
度して踊るのでありま
す。揚受と同じく、最
後は大きな氣合を掛け
て下さい。

（十八）

（八十）段初安平

第
二
十
圖

Picture Twenty

Step forward again with your right foot and strike with a left Chudan Oizuki. Initially, you walked down the Second Straight Line executing Jodan Age Uke, now you are returning down that same line doing Chudan Oizuki. Just like with the Age Uke, shout a powerful Kiai on the last strike.

平安初段（十七）

第二十圖

平安初段（十八）

（十七）更に右足を進めて、左中段追突を行ふ。

（十八）再び右足を進めて、右中段追突して、丁度上段揚受に依つて、前に進んだ第二線上を、中段追突を三度して踊るのであります。揚受と同じく、最後は大きな氣合を掛けて下さい。

第二十一圖

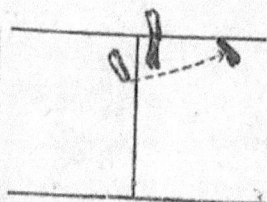

平安初段（十九）

第二十二圖

平安初段（二十一）

第二十三圖

（十九）右足を軸にして、左足を左第一線上に九十度廻轉し、右足を屈して後屈姿勢になり、左右の拳を開いて、兩手交叉しながら、反動を付けて手刀受の姿勢になります。

（二十）左第一線に、左足の位置から四十五度の角度の線上に、右足を一歩進めて、中段手刀受を行ふ。

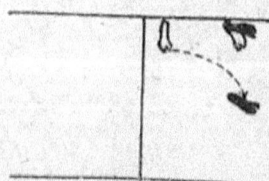

平安初段（二十）

（二十一）左足を軸にして、右足を再び百三十五度廻轉し、右第一線上に返し乍ら、三度後屈の中段手刀受を行ふ。

（二十二）左足を軸にして、右足を再び三十五度廻轉し、右第一線上上り乍ら、

Step Nineteen

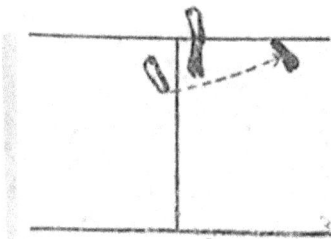

第
二
十
一
圖

第
二
十
二
圖

平安初段（九十）

（十九）右足を軸に
して、左足を左第一線
上に九十度廻轉し、右
足を屈して後屈姿勢に
なり、左右の拳を開い
て、兩手交叉しながら
反動を付けて手刀受の
姿勢になります。

Picture Twenty-One

Focus your weight on your right foot, rotate your body 90°counterclockwise and step on to the Left First Straight Line with your left foot. Allow your right knee to bend so you are in Kokutsu stance. Open both hands and bring them towards you, crossing them. Strike out again with a Shuto Uke.

Step Twenty

（二十）左第一線に、左足の位置から四十五度の角度の線上に、右足を一歩進めて、中段手刀受を行ふ。

（二十）段初安平

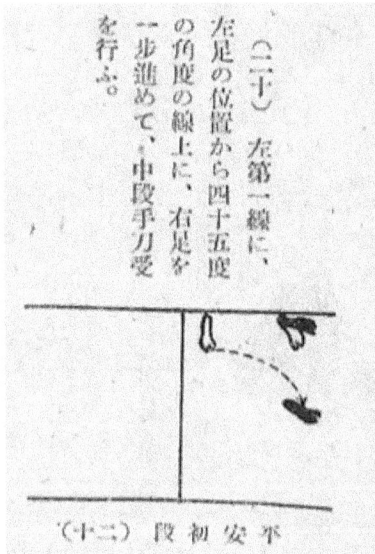

Picture Twenty-Two

Rotate your left foot 45°clockwise off the First Straight Line as you step forward with your right foot. Strike with a Chudan Shuto Uke.

Step Twenty-One

平安初段(二十一)

(二十一)左足を軸にして、右足を再び右第一線上に返し乍ら、三十五度廻轉し、右第一線上に返し乍ら、三度後屈の中段手刀受を行ふ。

Picture Twenty-Three

Placing your weight on your left foot and rotate clockwise 135° planting your right foot on top of the Right First Straight Line. You strike Chudan Shuto Uke for the third time in Kokutsu stance.

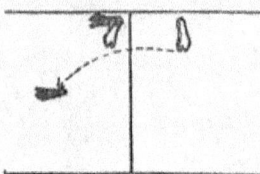

平安初段（二二）

第二十四圖

第二十五圖

第二十六圖

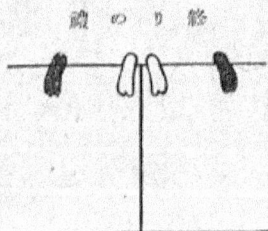

終りの禮

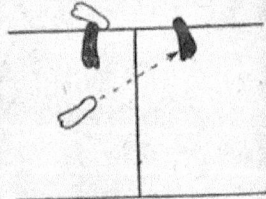

直れの姿勢

八字立から閉足にして、靜かに禮が終る迄は決して氣をゆるめない事が大切であります。

次に禮がすむと、用意の時の位置と、直れの時の位置をよく注意して下さい。最初に餝りの位置がくるふ樣ではいけません。

（注意）型の順序をよくおぼへる迄は出來るだけ輕く、形を正し、演武の方向を一定にせず、あらゆる方向に向つて練習して下さい。型が無意識に自由自在に出來る樣になりましたら、一擧手一蹴足に全精神を打込んで何囘も反復練習し、型の妙味を十分研究する事が大切であります。

○平安初段分解説明

平安初段を分解すると、前に述べました樣に五種の手の動作と三種の足取りからなつてゐます。

中段　直突　　右、四回　左、三回　前屈立
上段　揚受　　右、二回　左、一回　前屈立
下段　拂受　　右、二回　左、四回　前屈立
中段　打落　　右、一回　　　　　　レ字立
中段手刀受　　右、二回　左、二回　後屈立

此の五種類の技が如何なる武術的意義を持つものであるか證明致します。

下段拂受

下段拂受は内受と外受の二種ありまして、内受は敵が右足で蹴つて來た場合、我は右足を一步引きながら左拳で敵の足を内側から拂び受ける時は内受で、次に敵が同じく右足で攻撃して來た時、左足を一步引きながら右拳を以て外側から下段拂受した場合は外受であります。

（二四）（二三）の正反對に、第一線上の右足を軸にして、左足を進めて中段手刀受を行ふ。

（二五）左足を百三十五度第一線上に捻轉させ、兩手を握りながら、元の用意の姿勢に復します。

Step Twenty-Two

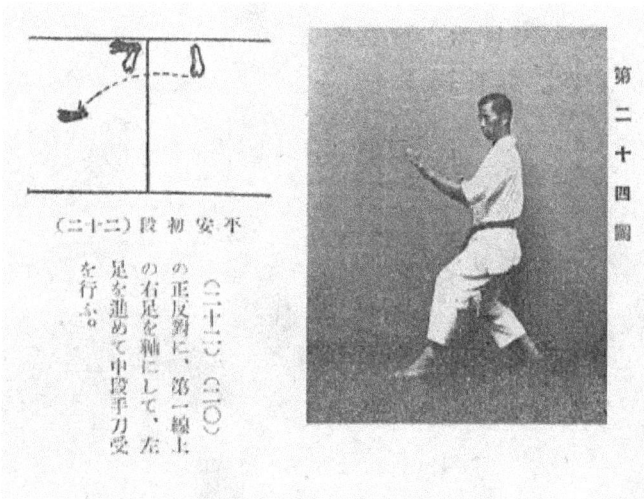

Picture Twenty-Four

This is the exact opposite of Step Twenty. Pivot on your right foot and step forward with your left foot. Strike with a Chudan Shuto Uke.

Step Twenty-Three

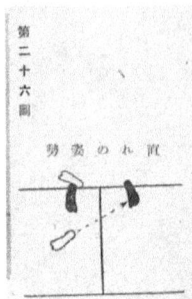

第
二
十
六
圖

直れの姿勢

Naore no Shise
Return to Start Position

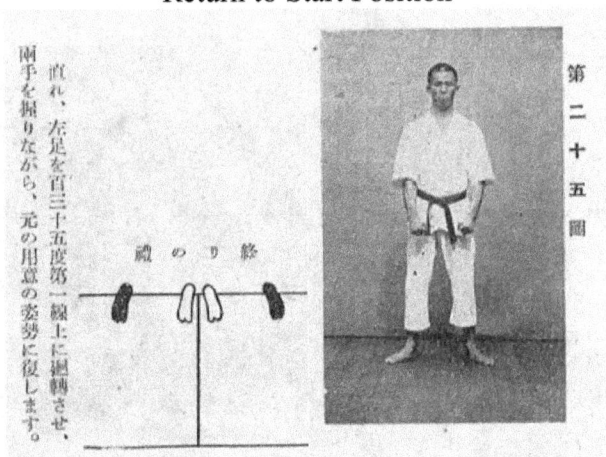

Picture Twenty-Five

Picture Twenty-Six

Owari no Rei
Final Bow

To return to the starting position rotate your left foot 135°and place it on the First Straight Line. While keeping your fists clenched, return to the Yoh-I, Ready Stance.

Naore

The movement of *Naore*, returning to your starting position, should be done slowly and calmly. From Hachimonji Dachi, standing with your feet like Hachi 八 the Kanji for eight, step inward so your feet are together. Silently do a bow and understand it is important that you maintain your fighting spirit all the way to the end.

After bowing, check that the spot where you took the Ready Stance and the spot where you Returned to Your Starting Position are the same. It is important that the place you start and the place you end are not different.

Cautions

Until you have memorized the steps in this Kata you should do the exercises slowly and without power, focusing on getting the proper movements. Don't always begin practicing this Enbu, martial arts demonstration, facing the same direction, but instead practice beginning from different directions.

Once you have become able to do the Kata freely without thinking about it at any place and at any time, fill each punch and each kick with the totality of your martial spirit as you strike. It is essential that you train this technique repeatedly until you have a thorough understanding of the Kata.

Heian Shodan Bunseki Setsumei
A Breakdown of Heian Shodan

○平安初段分解説明

平安初段を分解すると、前に述べました様に五種の手の動作と三種の足取りからなつてゐます。

中段　直突　　右、四回　　左、三回　前屈立
上段　揚受　　右、二回　　左、一回　前屈立
下段　拂落　　右、二回　　左、四回　前屈立
中段　打落　　右、一回　　　　　　　レ字立
中段手刀受　　右、二回　　左、二回　後屈立

此の五種類の技が如何なる武術的意義を持つものであるか説明致します。

下段拂受

下段拂受は内受と外受の二種ありまして、内受は敵が右足で蹴つて来た場合、我は右足を一歩引きながら左拳で敵の足を内側から拂ひ受けるものであります。次に敵が同じく右足で攻撃して来た時、右足を一歩引きながら右拳を以て外側から下段拂受した場合は外受であります。

（直れ）の動作はユツクり落着いて行ひ、周囲の八字立から閉足にして、静かに禮が終る迄は決して氣をゆるめない事が大切であります。次に禮がすむと、周囲の時の位置と、直れの時の位置をよく注意して下さい。最初に絞りの位置がくるふ様ではいけません。

（注意）型の順序をよくおぼへる迄は出来るだけ輕く、形を正し、演武の方行を一定にせず、あらゆる方行に向つて練習して下さい。焉が無意識に自由自在に出来る様になりましたら、一擧手一投足に全精神を打込んで何回も反復練習し、型の意味を十分研究する事が大切であります。

- Four right Chudan Choku Zuki and three times on the left. Zenkutsu Stance.

- Two right Jodan Age Uke and one on the left. Zenkutsu Stance.

- Two right Gedan Harai Uke and four on the left. Zenkutsu Stance.

- One right Chudan Uchi Otoshi. In Reiji Dachi, Standing Like the letter レ Rei.

- Two right Chudan Shuto Uke and two on the left. Kokutsu Stance.

Each of the five actions described above has an underlying martial arts meaning, defining a situation where you are attacked in a certain way. I will describe them now.

（指導）

第一圖の様に、敵が正面から我が腹部を攻撃し
て来た時、我は左足を一歩引いて、下段拂外受を
して、敵が蹴つた足を引く咄嗟に我は一歩足を進
めると同時に左拳で敵の水月を中段直突で攻撃す

第一圖

下段外拂受

る場合もありまして、平安初段の一、二、動作、
十、十一、動作、十二、十三、動作に十四、十五
の動作等が下段拂受の内、外受の意味でありま
す。

○下段拂受の應用

下段拂受は幾久通りにも應用出来ますが、其の
一例を示すと、第二圖のやうに敵が攻撃して来た
足を右下段拂外受をすると同時に、前に屈してゐ
た足で敵の金を攻撃します。この蹴り方は蹴足を
十分練習してゐないと、咄嗟の場合に自由に蹴る

第二圖

下段拂受の應用

事が困難であります。

○打落

平安三、四の動作打落は、敵が背側から足で攻
撃して来た時、第三圖のやうに右下段拂受を行ふ
と同時に、敵が攻撃した足を引いて、拂受した我
が右拳を掴む時に、我は前に屈した足を半歩程引
きよせながら、掴まへられた右拳は肘を曲げて
拳が左肩斜の所にとる、（第四圖参照）掴んだ
胸を足と共に急に引きはなされた爲に、敵の體が
前に崩れた刹那、腰を十分落しながら、すかさず
裏拳を以て、敵の顔面を攻撃する、（第五圖参照）
第三圖から第五圖迄を一擧動で行ひます。もし
敵が掴へた手を打落した瞬間、敵が後に體を退た

第三圖

打常（イ）

第四圖

打落（ロ）

Gedan Harai Uke

Picture One

There are two types, Uchi Uke, Inner Block, and Soto Uke, Outer Block. Use Uchi Uke when your opponent kicks. Respond by dropping your right foot back one step while using your left fist to strike your attacker's leg from the inside, blocking his attack and sweeping his leg away. This is how Uchi Uke is done.

Next, your opponent again kicks with his right foot. This time respond by dropping back with your left foot one step and using your right fist to strike the outside of your attacker's leg with a Gedan Harai Uke. This is how Soto Uke is done.

As Picture One shows, your attacker approaches from the front and launches his kick straight at your stomach. You respond by dropping your left foot back one step and defending with Gedan Harai Soto Uke. The moment your opponent pulls the leg he kicked with back, step forward with your left foot and punch to Suigetsu, the solar plexus, with Chudan Oizuki.

The first two movements in Heian Shodan as well as steps 10~11, 12~13, 14~15 are all Gendan Harai Uke on the inside or outside. This is the purpose of this strike.

Application of Gedan Harai Uke

Picture Two

While Gedan Harai Uke can be used in various ways, I will highlight one method here. As Picture Two shows, you have defended with your right fist against your attacker's right kick using a Gedan Harai Soto Uke. At the same time, you use your right foot, which is out in front, to kick your opponent in Kane, the groin.[21] If you do not train kicking in this manner extensively it will be a difficult attack to pull off in a sudden situation.

---

[21] Gigo Sensei uses the word *Kane* 金 Metal to refer to the groin. L: *A Collection of Karatedo* (1936) Tsurugane, Hanging Bells. R: *An Introduction to Karate*空手道入門 by Oya Reikichi (1951) calls it Kinteki (Tsurugane, Hanging Bell, Kogan, Testicles) and notes, "Striking this place can cause death. Attack with your fist, knee or a kick."

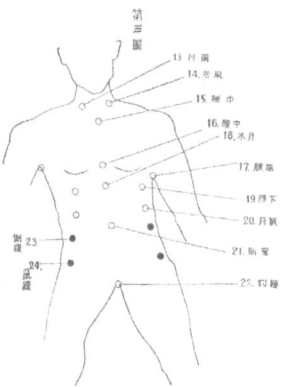

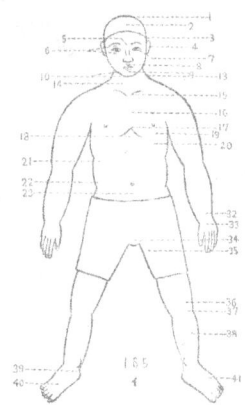

Uchi Otoshi

Picture Four

Picture Three

Picture Five

Uchi Otoshi

Movements 3~4 in Heian are Uchi Otoshi. Your opponent has attacked from behind with a kick and you respond with a right Gedan Harai Uke. Your attacker immediately withdraws the foot he kicked with and seizes your right hand, which you used to block his attack.
You respond by pulling your front foot a half-step back and freeing your right hand by bending your elbow and yanking it towards your left shoulder. This is shown in Picture Four.

Since you have stepped back and freed your arm by yanking it back at the same time, your opponent will lose his balance forward.

The moment this happens, while ensuring your hips are sufficiently low, immediately strike your opponent in the face with Ura Ken. This is shown in Picture Five.

Pictures 3~5 show one continuous movement. If your opponent drops back after you strike with a Uchi Otoshi, step forward with your left foot and strike him in Suigetsu, the solar plexus, with your left fist.

第五図

打　蔕　（ハ）

第×六図

上段揚受　（イ）

第七図

上段揚受　（ロ）

第八図

上段揚受　（ハ）

時は我は左足を進めて敵の水月を左拳で攻撃します。平安五動作

○上段揚受

上段揚受も下段拂受と同様に、内受外受と二種になつてゐます。つまり平安六、七の動作の様に、敵が右拳で攻撃した時我は右足を後に引いて左腕で受けた時は内で、その反對に左足を引いて右腕で受けた場合は外受になります。

第六図のやうに敵が、我が正面から顔面を右拳で攻撃した時、我は右足を一歩引きながら左上段受をなす。左手で敵の手首を摑んで左脇中に捻りながら引込むと同時に、右足を一歩踏込みながら逆になつた敵の腕を揚受する要領で打込むのであります。平安六、七の動作で一擧動で行ふ事が肝要です。

又今度は前と反對に、同じく敵が前にする刀で打つて來た時、右上段揚受をして、敵の手首を右脇下に捻り込むと同時に左拳を以て攻撃します。（第八図参照）

又上段揚受の應用として、敵が顔面を攻撃した際、敵の腕を逆に取つて打込まずに、上段に受けると同時に、構へた拳を敵の水月に攻撃する場合もあります。

○手刀受

手刀受は牢手の型に最もおほく出てくる型で、最初はかなり、ぎこちなく困難な受方ですが、稽古が積に從つて應用にとんでゐる受でありまして、此の手刀受も先の受け方と同じく、内、外の受方があります。第九図は手刀内受であります。普通

Jodan Age Uke

Picture Seven	Picture Six

Just like Jodan Age Uke, Gedan Harai Uke also has an inner and outer version. Specifically, in steps 6~7 of Heian, your attacker strikes with his right fist.

An Uchi, inner, response is when you step back with your right foot and block with your left arm. A Soto, outer, response is the opposite, you step back with your left and block with your right.

As Picture Six shows, the attacker aims a punch at your face with his right fist. You pull back your right foot while doing a left Jodan Uke, blocking this strike. Then seize your attacker's right wrist with your left hand and twist it, pulling his arm towards your left armpit. As you do this step forward with your right foot and lift up your opponent's arm, which you have in a joint lock. This is an outline of how to defend against a strike with Age Uke. It is essential that steps 6~7 of Heian be executed in one continuous movement.

Picture Eight

Next, the same technique on the opposite side. Your opponent tries to punch you in the face, the same as before. This time you respond with a right Jodan Age Uke, seize your opponent's wrist and twist it towards your right armpit. At the same time, strike with your left fist. This is shown in Picture Eight.

There are also other ways to respond with Jodan Age Uke. For example, after blocking your opponent's punch to your face, instead of grabbing his wrist and putting him in an armlock, you can use your other fist to punch him in Suigetsu, the solar plexus.

Shuto Uke

（尊　　指）

手刀受は中段受に使用してゐますが、時に依つては上段、下段にも應用してゐます。

第九圖

中段手刀受

第九圖の様に敬が胸部を攻撃して來た場合、我は一歩退つて、敬の腕を内から受けると同時に胸に構へた左手刀で、水月に貫手で攻撃する場合もあります。外受はその反になります。

Picture Nine

Shuto Uke is a block that appears the most frequently in Kata. It can feel a bit awkward blocking this way at first, however with sufficient training you will find it can be applied in many situations.

Shoto Uke is like the previous block in that it has an outer and inner version. Picture Nine shows Shuto Uchi Uke, Inner Block. Typically, Shuto Uke is used to defend against Chudan, attacks to the center of your body, but it can also be used for Jodan, attacks to your face, and Gedan, attacks to your lower body.

Picture Nine shows an attacker advancing and punching to your chest. You take one step back and use Shuto Uke to deflect the attack from the inside. At the same time use your left hand, which is ready in Kamae, to strike your opponent in Suigetsu, the solar plexus, with Nukite, Spear Hand. Soto Shuto Uke is done on the opposite side.

Karate Jutsu no Kankousho
A Reference Guide to Karate Techniques
By Funakoshi Gigo
Japanese Medical Newspaper
日本医事新報　#983
July 1941

寫真に關する參考書

空手術の參考書

手裏劒術の書籍

Karate Jutsu no Kankousho
A Reference Guide to Karate Techniques
By Funakoshi Gigo
Japanese Medical Newspaper
日本医事新報　#983
July 1941

QUESTION
　I would like to know about reference guides related to Karate Jutsu, the name of the publisher as well as the name of the author and the price. I would appreciate a simple explanation of those points.
(From a medical student in Miyagi Prefecture)

ANSWER
　Ka・ra・te, written with the Kanji "Chinese Hand" is a type of Chinese Kenpo transmitted to ancient Ryukyu. In Ryukyu it was simply known as "Te." As for the "Kara" part of the name, it is not clear if that refers to the term *Toshu Kuken*, Barehanded and Weaponless, or simply the Kanji "Empty," or even the Kanji "Chinese" to indicate the technique was transmitted from China. It seems likely that the word "Kara" is similar in meaning to "Kara-Imo" the "Chinese" sweet potatoes imported from Satsuma Domain, and other such products.
　According to oral tradition, Karate originated as a method of intense training done at Zen temples. It developed out of *Senzui* and *Ekikin*.[22]

---

[22] *Senzui* 洗髄 refers to a traditional Chinese method for training the body to discharge toxins to strengthen bones, internal organs, and muscles. This is done in order to project the wisdom from Buddha's mind (in other words, mental training.)
Ekikin is made up of two Kanji, the first means 易 Change and the second 筋 refers to strengthening the muscles of the body. Ekikin 易筋 is a series of mental and bodily exercises to cultivate Sei (Jing or essence) and direct and refine Ki (Qi,) the internal energy of the body. Thus, the overall meaning is to train your body until it is solid and strong (in other words physical exercise.)

This evolved into two schools: Shorei and Shorin. The name Shorin apparently originates from the Shorin temple in Henan Province, China. While there are no documents that record when this martial art was transmitted to Ryukyu, it seems likely it came over in the early Ming dynasty (1368~1644.) It is thought that after the armistice following the Keicho invasion of Ryukyu in 1609, the defeated warriors of Ryukyu worked to refine and perfect *Mute no Hiho*, a Secret Unarmed Method of Fighting, eventually succeeding in developing a unique fighting style.

In China, the strike known as *Tsuki* uses the tips of the fingers. On the other hand, striking with *Kenkotsu*, knuckles of the hand, was most likely a development unique to Ryukyu. The reason is because of the existence of the striking tool known as Makiwara, which clearly has no equivalent name in China.

Originally, there were a great many methods, however they were naturally reduced in number through refinement and now there are about twenty varieties that remain.

Long ago there were no ranks given in Karate. However recently as this art has developed and spread, a method of evaluating a person's training and certifying teachers has been developed. Now, at the Funakoshi Dojo there is a system of awarding Kyu ranks and Dan ranks to encourage students. In other words, there are two categories of rank: Kyu and Dan. There are seven Kyu ranks and eight Dan ranks. A year is also divided into four seasons, with each season being three months long. The year begins in April and ends in March.

The following three points will address Karate's value as a method of physical fitness. Every action is done with total focus of spirit, thereby enabling you to move extremely rapidly and nimbly. It not only encourages your circulatory system as well as your respiratory system to operate at an accelerated rate, but it also encourages the healthy expulsion of old matter and the intake of new,[23] thereby developing deftness of movement and the ability to have fine control over your body.

Karate contains more than a multitude of ways to exercise and apply the muscles of the legs. When training this systematic exercise method, you learn how to use different leg movements and positions in order to maintain your balance, as well as how to advance and

---

[23] *Shinjin Taisha* 新陣代謝 old things are expelled and new things are brought in.

retreat. As an exercise system that manipulates all points of the body, there are many aspects that are clearly beneficial.

A brief outline of Karate Jutsu techniques as well as language commonly used when training:

Ken no Nigiri Kata	-	How to Make a Fist
Tsuki Kata	-	How to Strike
Shite to Katsute	-	Death Dealing Strike & Lifegiving Strike
Ashi no Tachi Kata	-	How to Position Your Feet
Kaikayku Shisei	-	Standing with Legs Open
Zenkutsu to Kokutsu	-	Forward Stance and Back Stance
Kibadachi	-	Horseback Stance
Te Waza	-	Hand Techniques
Ukete	-	How to Make a Fist
Haraite	-	Sweeping Block
Nukite	-	Spear Hand
Sukuite	-	Scooping Hand
Gyakute	-	Wrist Lock
Uchite	-	Striking Block
Kakete	-	Hooking Block
Tsukamite	-	Seizing
Hikite	-	Pulling in Block
Urate	-	Reverse Block
Enpi	-	Elbow Strike
Hente	-	Changing Hand
Ashi Waza	-	Feet and Leg Techniques
Tobi Geri	-	Jump Kick
Mikazuki	-	Cresent Moon (Toe Kick to the Liver)
Hiza Zuchi	-	Knee Hammer
Kekomi	-	Side Kick
Kinteki	-	Attacking the Groin
Namigaeshi	-	Returning Wave
Sankaku Tobi	-	Three Way Jump
Gyaku Waza	-	Joint Locks
Tani Otoshi	-	Push off a Cliff
Batto	-	Topple
Saka Neji	-	Reversing the Screw
Jiki Daoshi	-	Topple Directly
Yari Dama	-	To Spear a Ball

More details can be found in the book *Karatedo Kyohan* by Funakoshi Gichin, published by Kobundo Book Store (Kyohashi Ward, 1-2 Kyohashi, Tokyo City.) The posted price is 2 Yen 50 Sen.

Answer by Funakoshi Gigo of the All-Nippon Karatedo Shotokan Dojo.

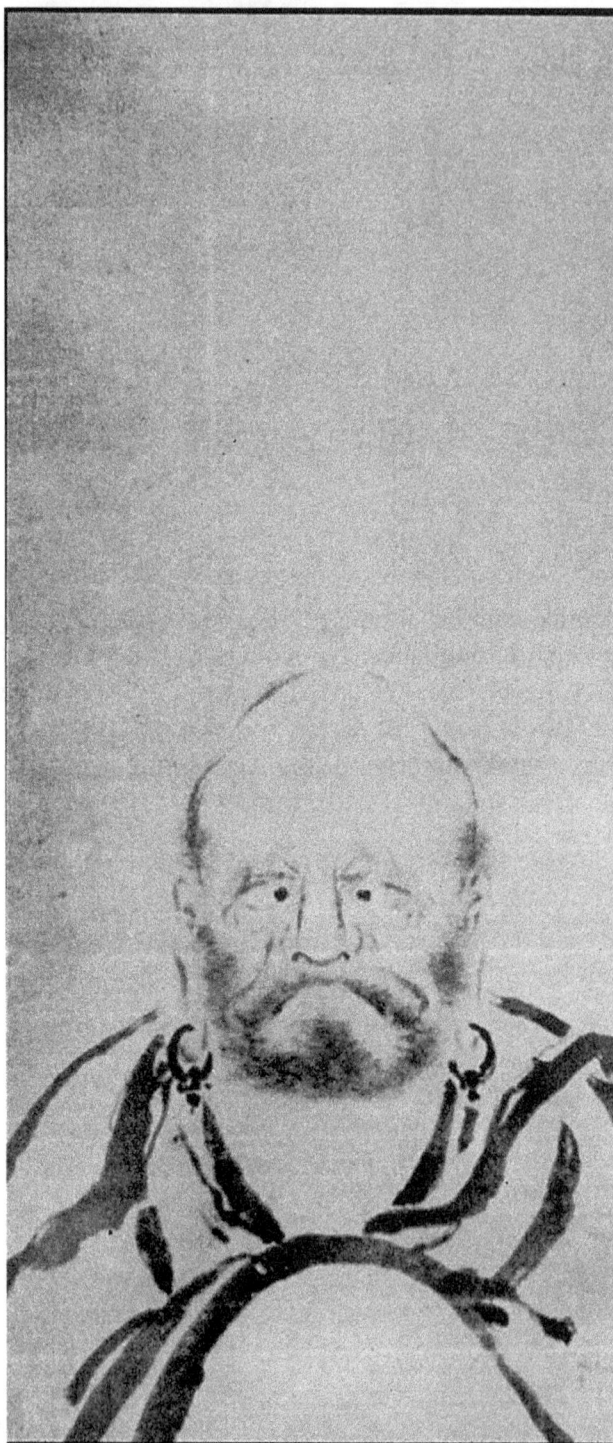

Painting of Daruma by Miyamoto Musashi

Ozeki Ryusuke (1907~1971) who authored several books on Japanese martial arts, records an episode with Funakoshi Gigo.

One day after training, the famous Karate practitioner Funakoshi Gigo, the son of Funakoshi Gichin, was preparing to leave the training space when one of his students gave a shout of *Ya!* and punched him from behind. Gigo Sensei simply jumped lightly to the side and spun around to face his student. He then said, *Try that punch again!*
The student gave a shout of *Iya!* and struck but he just lips back and his students fist stopped about five inches from his face.

This continued with the student punching and Gigo moving back just enough so his opponent's fist stopped five inches away. If the student jumped in three feet, Gigo would jump back three feet, if he jumped in four feet Gigo would jump back four feet. No matter what happened, the student's fist always ended up five inches in front of Gigo's face.

The student bowed in defeat and said, *How do you do it?*

Gigo replied, *This is known as "Discerning the distance" and it's something that martial artists from long ago trained extensively. Since I am able to judge almost the exact moment you are going to move, in addition to how far and how fast, all I have to do is simply move back a similar distance*

This is exactly like Miyamoto Musashi's *Maai no Mikiri*, discerning the distance between your opponent and yourself. Expanding on this, the art of sword is fundamentally about moving your body to a spot just out of reach of your opponent's sword tip and then use that understanding of distance to achieve victory. Musashi was a master of judging the distance between himself and an opponent.
It is thought that when Musashi fought Sasaki Kojiro this ability to clearly grasp the distance between himself and his opponent played a great part in his victory.

-Ozeki Ryusuke 尾関竜介
The Sword and Life 剣と人生
1969

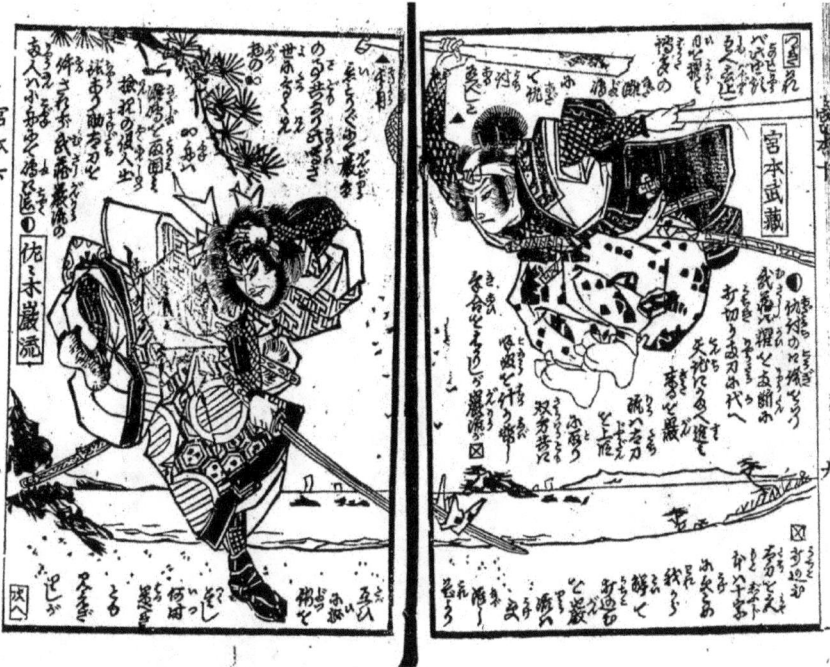

The 1716 book by Kumazawa Shotaro *Record of Samurai Generals'
Impressions* 武将感状記 contains a description of the final battle
between Sasaki Kojiro "Ganryu" and Miyamoto Musashi.

*Ganryu stepped forward and sliced horizontally across Musashi's
middle with his long sword.*
*Musashi leapt straight up, pulling his legs in close and Ganryu's
sword sliced 4 inches off the bottom of his Hakama. At the same time
Musashi gathered all his strength and struck Ganryu on the head with
both swords.*

As Ryusuke says in *The Sword and Life,*

> So, putting this simply, even if his Hachimaki headband is cut
> or his Hakama gets sliced, that doesn't mean that Musahi's
> Kenpo (way of the sword) is faulty, rather that is a fundamental
> part of Kenpo.

www.ingramcontent.com/pod-product-compliance
Lightning Source LLC
Chambersburg PA
CBHW070812280326
41934CB00012B/3160